Stonehenge

Julian Richards

Introduction

Today, visitors experience Stonehenge as a wonder of ancient achievement and an enduring symbol of mystery. But Stonehenge was built as a temple – a place of ceremony, of burial and of celebration. The first Stonehenge was simple – just a circular ditch and bank – and was constructed about 5,000 years ago, in the period of prehistory known as the Neolithic or New Stone Age.

By about 2500 BC timber structures had been built and rotted away and the first stones had started to arrive. Huge sarsen stones came from north Wiltshire and smaller bluestones from west Wales. This marked the beginning of over 800 years of construction and alteration stretching into the period known as the Bronze Age, when the first metal tools and weapons were made. By this time Stonehenge was the greatest temple in Britain, its banks, ditches and standing stones arranged in sophisticated alignments to mark the passage of the sun and the changing seasons. But Stonehenge was just one part of a remarkable ancient landscape. Hundreds of burial mounds clustered on the surrounding hilltops, while smaller temples and other ceremonial sites were built nearby. Stonehenge and these other ancient structures form an archaeological landscape so rich that it is classified as a World Heritage Site.

Stonehenge has inspired people to study and interpret it for centuries. Medieval writers used magic as an explanation of how it was created; antiquaries, like William Stukeley in the early 18th century, guessed – wrongly – that the Druids had built it. Archaeology provides the best hope of answering some of these fundamental questions about Stonehenge: how and when it was built, who built it and, perhaps most difficult of all, why it was built. But even with the evidence that archaeology and modern science provide, not all these questions can be answered. Stonehenge will always keep some of its secrets.

Above: Gold hair ornaments from about 2400 BC, some of the earliest gold objects found in the British Isles, from the burial of the Amesbury Archer, near Stonehenge

Facing page: Stonehenge seen here with the Slaughter Stone in the foregound. Never a sacrificial altar, this stone is simply a fallen upright in the entrance to the enclosure

Tour of Stonehenge

Although Stonehenge today is a hugely impressive ruin, it would have looked very different when it was first built. At first there were no central stones, only an earth ditch and banks and some small wooden posts or stone pillars. When stones were put up in the centre some remained in place but others were rearranged in different ways. The position of the stones today reflects only the last of these settings, and in the 20th century, after thousands of years of decay, some stones were also re-erected.

FOLLOWING THE TOUR

This tour of Stonehenge guides visitors around the site following the path that leads from the tunnel under the A344. Small numbered plans in the margins highlight stopping points and features of special interest. A tour of prehistoric monuments in the landscape around Stonehenge follows on page 20.

THE SITE

Stonehenge sits within a triangle of land bordered on two sides by busy roads. To the south is the A303, the main route from London to the South West. To the north lies the A344, which runs right past Stonehenge and cuts the main temple off from its landscape setting. This situation is not ideal, and there are plans for great improvements. The current approach to the stones is through a tunnel under the A344. From here, visitors follow a route that circles around the monument. The path crosses the outer ditch and bank and loops towards the central stones before recrossing the bank and ditch and completing the circuit. This allows visitors to view all parts of the site surviving above ground.

The most visible elements of Stonehenge are the stones themselves. Some are small, unshaped or broken, but many are massive, finely worked and intact. The central cluster has a jumbled appearance, but its stones were once arranged in a series of circular and horseshoe-shaped structures. Other stones, sitting in isolation near the inner edge of the bank, and in the entrance to the earthwork enclosure, had companions that have now vanished.

The earthworks enclosing Stonehenge have also changed. The ditches were dug from the chalk that underlies the site and the banks formed from the excavated material. When first dug they would have been gleaming white, but now, with the ditches largely filled in and the banks slumped and eroded, they are simply soft shapes in the grass. Other structures, revealed only briefly during excavations, are once again hidden from view. Under the grass, Stonehenge is dotted with hundreds of small holes, many of which once held an upright timber post. A circle of larger pits known as the Aubrey Holes, which originally held upright timbers or small stones, lies close to the inner edge of the bank. The positions of those that have been excavated are marked by pale concrete spots in the grass and on the path. Surrounding the central stones are two circles of smaller pits, known as the Y Holes and the Z Holes.

Together these structures of earth and stone, and the faint traces of timber, go to make up the ancient monument that we know as Stonehenge.

Left: Stonehenge in its present-day setting between two busy roads

Facing page: A great sarsen stone trilithon – two massive uprights capped by a horizontal lintel – one of five that stood at Stonehenge

Dating Stonehenge

Radiocarbon dating measures the amount of radioactive carbon in an archaeological sample. When calibrated against the radiocarbon content of tree rings with a known age, this can give very precise dates

All living things contain carbon, including a naturally radioactive form of carbon. When something dies, the carbon it contains decays gradually over time. Radiocarbon dating measures the amount of radioactive carbon remaining in an archaeological sample. When calibrated against the radiocarbon content of tree rings with a known age, this can give very precise dates for archaeological samples.

At Stonehenge, not all the individual events and structures could be dated, but radiocarbon dates were obtained for the antler picks used to dig the ditch and for a number of animal bones found at the bottom of the ditch.

This showed, with 95% probability, that the first phase of the monument was constructed between 3000 and 2920 BC, and that the animal bones were several hundred years older. Other carbon samples from the site have given dates for the early sarsen stone settings of about 2500 BC, and for the final bluestone settings of between 2300 to 2000 BC.

Right: Deer-antler picks used to dig the ditch, radiocarbon dated to between 3000 and 2920 BC

Below right: An ox jawbone found in the ditch, which gave a date several hundred years earlier than the antlers, and was probably buried as an offering (both the antler picks and jawbone are now in the Salisbury and South Wiltshire Museum)

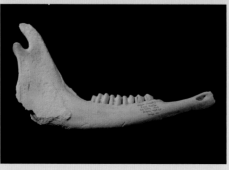

■ THE EARLY ENCLOSURE

The tunnel from the visitor centre emerges a little distance from the stones, outside the boundary formed by the circular ditch and bank. These earthworks are now grassed over, but are clearly visible as the path crosses over them on its way to the inner part of the monument. This is the first Stonehenge, constructed shortly after 3000 BC in the period known as the Neolithic or New Stone Age. In this, its first form, Stonehenge was similar to a number of other sites known as causewayed enclosures. Another example, Robin Hood's Ball, lies about a mile to the north-west.

The first Stonehenge was a roughly circular enclosure of about 110m (360ft) in diameter, defined by a ditch, an inner bank made of the chalk excavated from the ditch and, in places, a small outer bank known as a counterscarp. There were at least two entrances; one of these, still clearly visible today, faces north-east, towards the large stone by the roadside fence. This is the entrance that became the main way into the enclosure, but at this early stage in the construction of Stonehenge there was at least one other smaller entrance, on the southern side of the enclosure.

When Colonel William Hawley excavated much of the eastern side of Stonehenge in the 1920s, he found the silted-up ditch to be very irregular, varying considerably in width, depth and shape. Hawley likened it to 'a string of badly-made sausages'.

The ditch was originally dug using picks and rakes of red deer antler. The chalk to build the banks would most probably have been moved in baskets or skins. Fragments of these antler picks, thrown away or perhaps deliberately left on the ditch floor, have been radiocarbon dated to between 3000 and 2920 BC. But other, older bones were also found on the ditch floor. In the ends of some of the short segments of ditch, cattle bones, jaws and a skull had been carefully placed. When dated they turned out to be much older than the ditch, perhaps by as much as 300 years. These old bones must have been very special, perhaps offerings of some kind, left by the builders to mark the foundation of the new temple of Stonehenge.

Although we can be certain about when the enclosure was built, it is less certain what else of

Left: The stones seen from outside the bank and ditch to the north-west of the enclosure

Stonehenge was constructed at this time. One strong possibility is the circle of 56 circular pits, spaced between 4m and 5m (13ft and 16ft) apart, that lies just inside the inner edge of the bank. These pits are known as the Aubrey Holes after their original discoverer, the 17th-century antiquary John Aubrey (1626–97), who was one of the first to make systematic observations of Stonehenge.

Although 34 of the Aubrey Holes were excavated during the 20th century, not one provided samples that could be dated scientifically. It is also uncertain what stood in them: timber posts or small stone pillars. What the excavations did reveal was that the holes were used as places of burial, both when they contained the posts or pillars and after their removal. Cremated human bones were found, both in the Aubrey Holes and also in the bank and the ditch (which was by this time partly filled in). So, during its early life, Stonehenge was a cemetery, a place where the remains of the dead could be laid to rest. The cremated bones from Hawley's excavations, reburied in 1935 in an empty Aubrey Hole, were re-excavated in 2008. They appear to be the remains of about 60 individuals, almost entirely young male adults.

It is possible that some of the many other post holes for upright timbers, which have been found within the area enclosed by the bank and ditch, may also belong to this early stage of Stonehenge, before the large sarsen stones arrived.

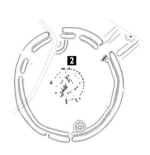

❷ THE SARSEN STONES AND BLUESTONES

In the form of its ditch and the animal bones that were carefully placed there, the first Stonehenge was not so different from many other enclosures of a similar date. Even cremated human bones have been found at other sites of this date. What made Stonehenge so unusual is what happened next: the arrival of the stones.

Moving within the earthwork formed by the ditch and bank and closer to the central stones, it is immediately obvious that they fall into two different groups in terms of their size. Many of the stones are very large, including the uprights closest to the path and, further in towards the centre, the pairs of uprights that support horizontal lintels. Others, nestled amongst the larger stones, are much smaller, some less than the height of an adult. These two groups of stones are quite different, both in their size and in the type of raw material from which they are formed.

The largest stones, some of which weigh over 40 tonnes, are known as sarsens. Sarsen is a type of extremely hard sandstone, small boulders of which can be found in the area around Stonehenge. But for larger sarsens the closest source lies more than 30km (19 miles) to the north of Stonehenge, on the Marlborough Downs in north Wiltshire. Here massive stones can still be seen half-buried in the bottoms of shallow valleys, although many others have been broken up for building material or cleared away to make cultivation easier.

The smaller stones at Stonehenge are known collectively as bluestones, although this group includes a variety of different types of rock. What unites them is their source, in the Preseli Hills of Wales, over 240km (150 miles) to the west of Stonehenge. There is no doubt about their origin: the mineral composition of stones from Stonehenge can be matched precisely with samples from Preseli.

It is difficult to explain the peculiar mixture within the bluestone group, but perhaps it represents not simply a collection of building materials, but the components of an existing stone circle that stood in Wales before being uprooted and brought to Stonehenge. There were originally at least 80 bluestones at Stonehenge, some weighing up to five tonnes.

So how did both types of stone get to Salisbury Plain? The sarsens are bigger, but are found closer to Stonehenge, and experiments have shown that stones this size can be dragged on a simple wooden sledge running on wooden rails by a team of about 200 people. To drag a stone from the Marlborough Downs to Stonehenge, using a route avoiding steep slopes wherever possible, would take about 12 days.

In the past there have been suggestions that the bluestones were found lying on Salisbury Plain where they had been carried by the movement of glaciers during the last Ice Age. There is little geological evidence to support this idea and it is now generally accepted that it was human rather than glacial transport that moved them. Although the bluestones are smaller, they had much further to travel and their route is still open to debate. The first part of their journey would have been by land, but water transport may also have been important. The river Avon, which flows close to Stonehenge, is often suggested as forming the final part of the bluestones' journey from Wales.

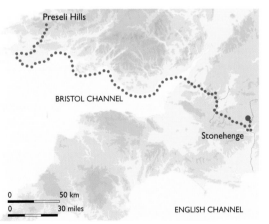

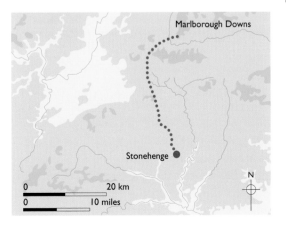

Left: Map showing one possible route by which the bluestones may have been transported to Stonehenge

Below: Map showing the likely route of the sarsen stones to Stonehenge

Facing page: The circles of sarsens and bluestones, showing the contrasting sizes of the two different types of stone

Above: Part of the outer sarsen circle with the best preserved section of surviving lintels, seen from the north-east

Below: An elegantly grooved stone in the bluestone horseshoe, possibly intended to be jointed to a similar stone with a corresponding tongue

▣ THE STONE SETTINGS

Moving further along the path, parallel with the central stones, visitors get a clear view of the way in which the larger sarsens have been shaped and fitted together. At most stone circles built at this time in prehistory, blocks of stone were left in their natural, rough state and simply raised upright, but at Stonehenge they were treated differently. The sarsens within the central settings have been carefully trimmed, sometimes to produce sharply defined rectangular blocks, and have also been shaped to produce simple joints that lock the stones tightly together. Some of the bluestones also show evidence of shaping and jointing, although in their current setting they all seem to have been freestanding.

What can be seen today are the ruins of the stone settings that were constructed over several centuries from about 2500 to 2000 BC. Once in place the huge sarsens do not appear to have been moved but, in contrast, the smaller bluestones may have been rearranged several times.

There are four concentric settings, two circles and two of horseshoe shape. Even after more than 4,000 years of decay, these structures can still be recognized today. The outermost setting was originally a circle of 30 upright sarsens, capped by horizontal lintel stones. Of these 30 uprights only 17 still stand while only five of the lintels are still in place, leaving the best preserved section on the north-eastern side, facing the entrance to the enclosure. The surviving uprights are closely spaced, with gaps of less than 1.5m (5ft) between the stones; there is a slightly wider gap between those that most directly face the main entrance.

The uprights and the lintels are locked together by means of a joint more commonly used in woodworking: the mortise and tenon. A protruding peg, or tenon, on the top of each upright fits into a corresponding hole, or mortise, hollowed out of the underside of the lintel. The ends of the lintels are locked together by tongue and groove joints (also derived from carpentry), where a vertical tongue fits into a corresponding vertical groove. The sophistication of this part of the structure is increased by the shaping of the horizontal lintels: these are not rectangular as might be expected, but gently curved on both inner and outer faces. If this outer circle – now much ruined – was ever complete, its lintels would

have formed a perfect ring of stone suspended high and perfectly level above the ground.

Inside and concentric with these sarsens lay a circular setting of as many as 60 small, upright bluestones, the majority of which show no sign of having been worked or shaped. Within this circle, though, are two finely worked stones with mortise holes which were clearly shaped as horizontal lintels before being reused as upright pillars. This circle is now fragmentary.

Moving inwards, the next setting was the most impressive: a horseshoe of five massive sarsen trilithons (from the Greek for 'three stones'). Each trilithon consisted of two huge closely spaced uprights and an equally huge horizontal lintel, locked together with mortise and tenon joints. Three complete trilithons still stand (although the one closest to the tarmac path was re-erected in 1958). Among their uprights are the biggest individual stones at Stonehenge, weighing well over 40 tonnes. As rough stones when first found, before they were so carefully shaped, they must have weighed considerably more. This sarsen horseshoe is an extremely sophisticated structure, as the individual trilithons were originally graded in

height, with the tallest, known as the Great Trilithon, at the closed end of the horseshoe. Only one stone of this magnificent structure still stands, the tallest standing stone in Britain, over 7.3m (24ft) high. Some of the trilithon uprights were decorated with carvings of daggers and axes made over 700 years after they were raised.

The innermost setting is another horseshoe, this time of bluestone pillars. There were originally 19 stones, larger than those in the bluestone circle and including a number that were elegantly shaped. Some bear evidence that they once had tenons, suggesting that they supported lintels, although not where they stand today.

Finally, at the closed end of the innermost horseshoe, in the shadow of the tallest trilithon and now partly buried beneath its fallen upright, lies a stone known as the Altar Stone. This is the largest of the non-sarsen stones, a greenish sandstone from south Wales.

Not only were the stones carefully shaped and jointed together but the two horseshoes, of sarsen and bluestone, were lined up precisely so that their open ends pointed directly towards the entrance to Stonehenge.

Above left: The tallest stone at Stonehenge, the surviving upright of the Great Trilithon, which formed part of the sarsen horseshoe; note the prominent tenon

Above right: One of the three surviving trilithons from the central sarsen horseshoe

Below: Diagram showing the joints used on the outer sarsen circle, with a mortise and tenon joint locking the uprights to the lintels and a tongue and groove joint locking the lintels together end-to-end

Top: A collection of sarsen hammerstones, or mauls, found at Stonehenge (now in the Salisbury and South Wiltshire Museum)

Above: Carvings of prehistoric daggers on an upright of one of the sarsen trilithons, probably dating from about 1800 BC

Below: Diagrams showing one possible way in which the standing stones may have been raised to an upright position

◀ RAISING THE STONES

As the path leads back over the bank and ditch, note the pale concrete spots in the grass that mark the position of excavated Aubrey Holes. The path then curves left round the outside of the enclosure.

Having moved their building materials to Stonehenge, how did our prehistoric ancestors shape and erect these stones? Although Stonehenge was constructed during a time when stone tools were gradually being replaced by copper and bronze, these new metals were too soft to have been used to shape the hard sarsens or bluestones. Both types of stone could only have been shaped by using round sarsen balls known as mauls. Many have been found at Stonehenge, ranging from the size of an orange to some as big as footballs. Shaping the stones, and creating the joints that fixed them together, must have been a long and uncomfortable process. Evidence, in the form of layers of stone chippings, suggests that the main sarsen working area lay just to the north of the enclosure, on the opposite side of the modern road. Once shaped, the stones intended as uprights could be raised. Holes were dug into the chalk, the depth of each one calculated in order to level up the tops of the stones (it was easier to dig out chalk than to remove bits from the stone).

Excavation has shown that most of the holes that hold uprights have one straight side and one that slopes. It seems likely that the stone was slid into the hole and initially rested at an angle against the sloping side. Experiments have shown that this can be done by balancing the stone on a ramp, with its end poised over the hole. Smaller stones can then be dragged along the length of the stone until their weight causes it to overbalance, pivot on the solid end of the ramp

and drop into the hole. The stone is then hauled upright against the vertical face using ropes of hide or vegetable fibre. Finally the hole is backfilled with chalk, fragments of stone, bits of broken deer antler picks and mauls, all rammed down firmly to hold the stone in place.

There are several theories as to how the lintels were raised into position. Experiments have shown that a 10-tonne stone can be dragged sideways up a sloping ramp made of earth or timber. Alternatively the lintels could have been raised on a platform of interlocking timbers. Each end of the lintel would have been raised in turn, using levers. As each end was levered up, supporting timbers would have been inserted and the stone rose as the platform grew in height. Either of these methods is possible and would have left no trace for archaeologists to find.

Most of what is carved on the surface of the stones is of a recent date – the names of visitors who must have come prepared with a hammer and chisel; but some decoration is much older. The shallow outlines of daggers and axes of prehistoric form lay undiscovered until spotted by a sharp-eyed archaeologist in 1953. These carvings cannot be directly dated, but the shapes of the weapons and tools suggest that they date to later in the Bronze Age, about 1800 BC.

THE AXIS OF STONEHENGE

This is a good point from which to view the main alignment, or axis, of the whole temple (see page 17). Look past the tallest surviving upright with its pronounced tenon, through the stones and out towards the enclosure entrance, marked by the Heel Stone by the side of the road. This is the direction in which the sun rises at midsummer.

Experiments show that the upright stones could have been raised using a ramp with a pivot stone and stone weights.

The weights are pulled along the length of the stone, causing it to tilt forwards into the prepared hole.

As the stone tilts, the edge of its wooden sledge rests on the angle of the pivot stone, preventing the stone slipping.

The stone weights fall away from the upright and it comes to rest with its base in the hole.

Once the stone has been pulled upright, using ropes, the hole is packed firmly to stop the stone slipping back.

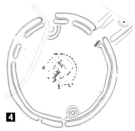

Left: Archaeologists Richard Atkinson and Stuart Piggott excavating at Stonehenge in 1958. Note the complex pattern of stone holes and post holes, revealed by the removal of the trilithon that fell in 1797

Below: Diagrams showing how the lintel stones may have been raised into position

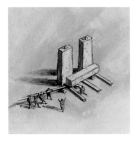

This is one way in which the lintel stones may have been raised, using timbers and wooden levers.

The lintel is supported on a timber platform which is gradually built up around both uprights.

Each end of the lintel is raised in turn using levers. As it is raised, more timbers are added to the platform.

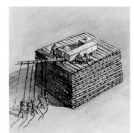

When the platform nears the top of the uprights, ropes are attached to the levers to exert downwards pressure.

Finally, when the frame is almost the same height as the uprights, the lintel can be levered into place.

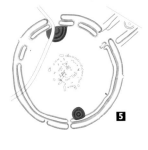

5 THE STATION STONES AND SOUTH AND NORTH BARROWS

As the path continues around the perimeter of the enclosure, it passes a small sarsen stone close to the inner edge of the bank. This is one of four known as the Station Stones that originally stood on roughly the same line as the Aubrey Holes. Of the four, two still survive: one upright, the other fallen, and both showing some small signs of having been shaped. The two missing stones were each surrounded by a circular ditch, creating the appearance of low mounds that became known as the North and South Barrows. Despite this name they are not burial mounds.

The Station Stones were most probably put in place at the same time that the central sarsen stones were raised, and their precise position was very carefully calculated. They mark the corners of a perfect rectangle with its central point in the exact centre of the monument. The reason for this is uncertain, although it has been suggested that the Station Stones were survey markers for the original builders.

It is important to remember that there are other elements of Stonehenge that can no longer be seen on the ground: structures of timber and arrangements of pits that have only been rediscovered by excavation. The Aubrey Holes, discovered by John Aubrey in the 17th century and excavated by Colonel William Hawley in the early 1920s, have already been mentioned. But there were two other circles of pits, both of which lay closer to the central stone settings. Colonel Hawley discovered these in 1923 and they were named the Y Holes and the Z Holes. Each circle originally consisted of 30 pits, oblong and about 1m (3ft) deep. They appear to have been dug late in the period of Stonehenge's construction, almost as an afterthought, but there is no evidence that they ever held uprights of stone or timber, so their purpose is unknown.

THE LANDSCAPE OF STONEHENGE

The path round the outside of the enclosure offers visitors a good view of the wider landscape. Stonehenge lies at the heart of an area rich in archaeology, within which are several more henges and other ceremonial sites, traces of prehistoric settlements, fields, boundaries, flint-working sites and, perhaps most obvious, burial mounds.

On every hilltop visible from Stonehenge there are low grassy mounds, some within woodland, others fenced or unfenced within fields. These are round barrows, each the burial place of someone of wealth and status in the early part of the Bronze Age, the time when the building of Stonehenge was nearing its completion. The position of these barrows is quite deliberate, many of them strung out along the crests of low ridges where they would have been most visible and most able to advertise the power of the people who lay beneath them. When first built, their mounds of chalk, dug out from a surrounding ditch, would have gleamed white against the grass.

The landscape surrounding Stonehenge contains one of the highest concentrations of Bronze-Age round barrows in the country. The mounds that can be seen today have survived centuries of landscape change that saw the deliberate destruction of many barrows and the gradual erosion, through ploughing, of many more. Originally there were more than 300 round barrows within a 3km (2-mile) radius of Stonehenge. This was a huge attraction for antiquaries and early archaeologists in the 18th and 19th centuries, with the result that nearly every barrow that can be seen has been at least partially excavated at some point in its history.

Many of the magnificent finds of pottery, amber, bronze and gold can be seen in the Wiltshire Heritage Museum in Devizes and the Salisbury and South Wiltshire Museum in Salisbury. Much of the surrounding landscape can also be explored on foot from Stonehenge (see page 29).

Below: Early Bronze-Age pottery vessels discovered in barrows close to Stonehenge (now in the Wiltshire Heritage Museum, Devizes)

Facing page: One of the massive inner sarsen trilithons, with a bluestone in the foreground

Lichens

Many of the lichen species found at Stonehenge usually grow only on exposed coastlines: their presence at Stonehenge remains mysterious

Even from a distance, visitors to Stonehenge can see that the surfaces of the stones do not have a uniform appearance. They are mottled with a wide variety of colours, created by different species of lichen covering virtually every exposed surface.

Every lichen consists of a fungus and a green alga (or a cynobacterium), living together in a mutually beneficial – or symbiotic – association. The algal partner contains chlorophyll and, like plants, has the ability to convert the sun's energy into sugar. The fungal partner constitutes the body of the lichen, protecting the alga from the harsh environments in which lichens live. Most lichens grow very slowly, increasing by between 0.5 and 5mm (0.02 and 0.2in) a year, depending on the species.

Lichens can be found in every climatic zone throughout the world, from arctic tundra to tropical rainforests, though each species is adapted to a specific type of environment.

A lichen survey at Stonehenge in 2003 found that there were 77 different species growing on the stones, several of which are nationally rare or scarce. Although it is hard to date lichens, as new growth is constantly replacing old, it will have taken hundreds of years for this range of species to become established on the stones. The lichen types at Stonehenge are broadly similar to those at the nearby stone circle at Avebury, but with some interesting exceptions.

Buellia saxorum, a type of lichen that specializes in colonizing sarsen stones and which is widespread at Avebury, is totally absent from Stonehenge for no apparent reason. Equally surprising, many of the lichen species found at Stonehenge usually grow only on exposed coastlines. It is possible that the prevailing winds at Stonehenge, blowing in from the Atlantic, may have encouraged these species to grow, but again, specialists have not been able to find a convincing explanation. So not all the mysteries of Stonehenge are archaeological.

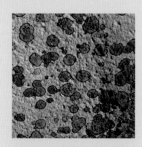

Above: Some of the lichens found at Stonehenge, including one (bottom) colonising an area where graffiti was cleaned off

⑥ THE HEEL STONE, SLAUGHTER STONE AND AVENUE

Moving further round the path, the visitor comes to a huge unworked sarsen, known as the Heel Stone, that stands close to the fence at the edge of the A344 road.

Today the Heel Stone stands in isolation, just outside the main entrance to the earthwork enclosure, surrounded by a small circular ditch. But it originally had a companion stone, the hole for which was discovered in the roadside verge in 1980. There are hints that the Heel Stone may have been found lying close to where it stands and not transported from the Marlborough Downs. From the Heel Stone the twin parallel banks and ditches of the Avenue run out across the downs, although today they are unfortunately cut off from Stonehenge by the road.

The route of the Avenue, which is interpreted as a ceremonial approach way to Stonehenge, starts on the bank of the river Avon at West Amesbury, over 2.5km (1.5 miles) away to the south-east. From here it curves up across the A303 road before crossing the tree- and barrow-covered ridge to the east and running down into a shallow valley. Here it turns and the final section runs straight for a distance of over 500m (550yds) up to the entrance to the enclosure.

This final section of the Avenue is just visible in the field on the opposite side of the road, particularly in low sunlight. The Avenue was probably constructed at the same time as, or just after the great stone structures were completed just before 2500 BC.

Turning away from the Heel Stone back towards the centre of Stonehenge, visitors can see another stone lying in the entrance to the enclosure. This is known as the Slaughter Stone, its gruesome name a product of overactive Victorian imagination.

The Slaughter Stone originally stood upright and, like the Heel Stone, was flanked by additional stones that are now missing. The surviving stone now lies horizontal, and shallow depressions on its surface collect rain water which reacts with iron in the stone and turns a rusty red. This was thought to be evidence of sacrifice – a relic of ancient blood spilt on a stone altar – hence the stone's lurid but highly inaccurate name.

THE ALIGNMENT OF STONEHENGE

This point, close to the Heel Stone, lies on the axis of Stonehenge. This is an alignment that runs north-east to south-west, up the final straight section of the Avenue and through the enclosure entrance. Recent excavations have shown that this part of the Avenue may be based on natural landscape features – 'visible stripes' in the surface of the chalk formed at the end of the last Ice Age. Within the central stones the alignment runs through the open ends of the horseshoes of sarsen and bluestone to where the Altar Stone lies at the base of the Great Trilithon.

This axis was carefully chosen because it reflects the annual movements of the sun. At Stonehenge on the longest day of the year, about 21 June in the modern calendar, the sun rises behind the Heel Stone in the north-east part of the horizon and its first rays shine into the heart of Stonehenge. This alignment is deliberate; it is shared with many other henges – temples of earth and wood – that were built around the same time. Close to Stonehenge there are two good examples, Coneybury to the south-east and Woodhenge to the north-east. The careful way that Stonehenge is laid out is seen as evidence that it was designed to mark and, presumably, celebrate the middle point of summer – the summer solstice. But an alignment that marks a midsummer event in one direction can also point to a midwinter event.

Because of the way the sun moves through the sky during the course of the year, the sunset at the winter solstice, the shortest day of the year, occurs on exactly the opposite side of the horizon from the midsummer sunrise. Observers at Stonehenge at the winter solstice (about 21 December), standing in the enclosure entrance and facing the centre of the stones, can watch the sun set in the south-west part of the horizon, just to one side of the only remaining upright of the Great Trilithon.

When this magnificent structure stood intact this effect would have been dramatic, the setting sun dropping rapidly down the narrow gap between the two upright stones. So Stonehenge may have been built to commemorate not so much the longest day, the summer solstice, but the shortest day, the solstice in the depths of winter. But why?

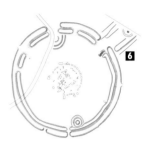

Above left: Stonehenge at midsummer sunset
Left: The Heel Stone, one of two sarsens that once stood just outside the main entrance to the enclosure, framed by the outer sarsen circle
Below: Diagram showing the alignment of Stonehenge with the midsummer sunrise and midwinter sunset

Overleaf: Midwinter – snow picks out the ditches of the Avenue in the approach to Stonehenge

Midsummer sunrise

Midwinter sunset

WHY WAS STONEHENGE BUILT?

This is the most difficult question for archaeology to answer. Stonehenge does not appear to have any obvious practical purpose. It was not lived in and could not have been defended, so it is thought there must have been a spiritual reason why Neolithic and Bronze-Age people put so much effort into building it.

These people were farmers, their survival dependent on the success of their crops and animals, and for them winter would have been a time of fear – dark months when days grew shorter and colder and when food supplies grew low. There would have been a longing for the return of the light and warmth that meant crops would grow and animals would feed and thrive. Light meant life. This may be a reason why Stonehenge was built and aligned so carefully: to mark not the longest day of the year but the shortest. This, the winter solstice, was the turning of the year, after which light and life would return to the world.

But there may be other reasons. At some time, perhaps early in its long history Stonehenge was a place of the dead, where cremated human bones were buried. It has even been suggested that the standing stones represent long dead ancestors, in contrast to the posts of the timber circles that represented the houses of the living.

Clues may also lie in the mysterious bluestones, transported all the way from Preseli in Wales, where there are folk tales told about their healing powers, tales that may have their origins far back in prehistoric times. So a belief in the healing powers of these stones may be a reason why so much effort went into moving them over such a great distance.

Stonehenge can perhaps be seen as the prehistoric equivalent of a great cathedral, like that at nearby Salisbury, built for worship and as a place where believers could come to find healing and hope and where important people could be buried.

But what took place at Stonehenge at special times of the year? Were there ceremonies, simple or elaborate? Were the stones decorated with paint or garlanded with flowers? Were there songs and dancing, processions and feasting? These are secrets that Stonehenge still keeps – archaeology cannot provide the answers.

The Druids

The ancient Druids were priests of the Iron Age who emerged more than a thousand years after Stonehenge was abandoned. The idea that the Druids built Stonehenge was reasonable, but wrong

It is a commonly held belief that Stonehenge was built by the Druids. This is not the case. Today's Druids are a 19th-century reinvention, but there were real ancient Druids: priests who flourished in the Iron Age, the centuries just before the Roman occupation of Britain in AD 43.

The association between Stonehenge and the Druids is due to the writings of 17th- and 18th-century antiquaries, including William Stukeley (1687–1765).

Stukeley was fascinated by Stonehenge and correctly deduced that it was built not by the Romans or Danes but by the people who lived in Britain before the Romans arrived. He also recognized it as a temple. Temples need priests and the only ancient priests Stukeley knew of were the Druids described by Roman writers. Stukeley's assumption that the Druids built Stonehenge was reasonable, but wrong. The Druids did not in fact emerge until more than a thousand years after Stonehenge was abandoned.

Right: Detail from an engraving showing William Stukeley as a Druid, from his book, Stonehenge, a Temple Restor'd to the British Druids *(London, 1740)*

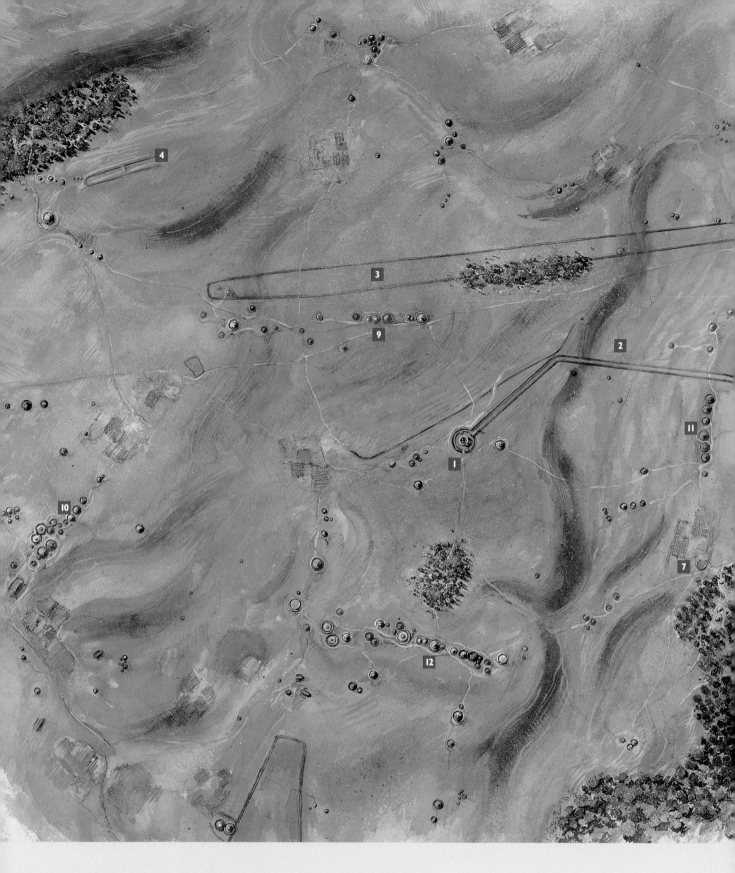

IMPORTANT LANDSCAPE FEATURES AROUND STONEHENGE

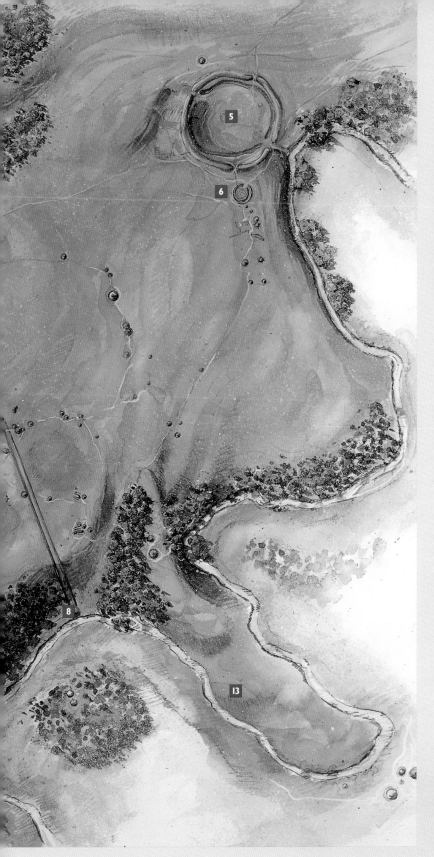

Landscape Tour

Stonehenge lies at the centre of a landscape so rich in prehistoric remains that it is classed as a World Heritage Site. The archaeological importance of this setting was recognized as far back as the 18th century, but until the early 20th century it appeared to contain only sites concerned with burial and ceremony. The advent of flying enabled photographs to be taken from the air, revealing traces of small farmsteads, boundary ditches, fields and trackways. Suddenly signs of everyday life in prehistory were visible.

In recent years more evidence for prehistoric life has come from 'field-walking' – the systematic collection of artefacts from the surface of ploughed fields. Shattered flint flakes reveal where flint was mined and tools were made while burnt stones and broken pottery reveal where people lived.

More recently a major campaign of excavations across the landscape has revealed far more about how the landscape developed at the time that Stonehenge was being built.

THE STONEHENGE WORLD HERITAGE SITE
In 1986 Stonehenge and Avebury were jointly inscribed on the World Heritage list for the outstanding prehistoric monuments at, and surrounding, both sites. The Stonehenge World Heritage Site covers 2,600 hectares, parts of which are owned by English Heritage, the National Trust, the Ministry of Defence and local farmers and householders. See page 29 for a map and access information.

Above: This painting shows the area around Stonehenge as it may have appeared in about 1600 BC, by which time all the main monuments in the area were already in place. At this point the later, more elaborate round barrows, such as disc barrows and saucer barrows, had joined the earlier long barrows and henge monuments, and at Stonehenge itself the Y and Z Holes had just been completed

ROBIN HOOD'S BALL

Robin Hood's Ball is an earthwork enclosure lying on the summit of a low ridge 4km (2.5 miles) north-west of Stonehenge. It lies in the Army's Salisbury Plain Training Area and is not accessible to the public. Consisting of two concentric circuits of ditch and bank, it is an example of a type of site known as a causewayed enclosure. Most were constructed in the earlier part of the Neolithic or New Stone Age, in about 3600 BC, but some may have remained in use for several centuries. Their name reflects the way in which their ditches were dug, not in a continuous circuit, but in a series of short segments separated by causeways. The first Stonehenge, the simple earthwork with its irregular ditch, is a late example of a site of this type.

Causewayed enclosures can have one, two or three circuits of ditch and a wide range of functions. Some appear to have been defensive sites; others were lived in; but the majority, like Robin Hood's Ball, appear to have been ceremonial. Their ditches often contain deliberately and carefully buried deposits of pottery – among the earliest to be found in Britain – and animal bones, perhaps the remains of feasts.

THE CURSUS

Built before the first Stonehenge was the unusual monument known as the Cursus. This is an elongated earthwork enclosure with a ditch and bank that define an area more than 100m (330ft) wide and 2.7km (1.7 miles) long. It runs east–west across the downland to the north of Stonehenge, crossing a shallow valley towards its central part.

The ditches on its long sides are small, little over 1m (3ft) deep, but both ends appear to

have been defined by larger ditches and correspondingly larger banks. Its eastern end stops just short of a levelled Neolithic long barrow.

It was first noted by the early 18th-century antiquary William Stukeley, who decided it was Roman in date and had been built for racing chariots or horses (hence the names he gave it, Cursus or Hippodrome, both Classical words for racetracks). He was wrong about the date: it was built in the early Neolithic period in about 3500 BC, but its function still remains uncertain. The few finds from the ditches suggest that it may have been laid out as a special or sacred space, perhaps for processions or as a barrier across the landscape. The entire length of the Cursus lies on National Trust open access land. The western end has been partially reconstructed.

THE LESSER CURSUS

Considering that they are rare monuments, it is remarkable that there is a second Cursus within the Stonehenge landscape, just to the north-west of the western end of the main Cursus. This one is much smaller, only about 400m (430yds) long, and is known as the Lesser Cursus. Excavations carried out in 1983 revealed that when first built, it was only half this length, but was extended shortly afterwards. Strangely, at its eastern end the ditches simply stop, leaving an open end, as if it was never completed. The newly dug ditches were then quickly filled in again, in one area covering a collection of antler picks neatly laid out in a line on the ditch floor. Radiocarbon dates from these picks suggest that the Lesser Cursus was also built in about 3500 BC.

LONG BARROWS

There are also many Early Neolithic long barrows in the Stonehenge area. These are elongated burial mounds, often flanked by ditches that acted as quarries for the chalk to build the mounds. Long barrows often contain the remains of many individuals, sometimes lying within wooden structures: symbolic houses for the dead. These are the tombs of the ancestors, raised not simply to contain bones, but as a way of establishing a claim to the land on which they stand. A large and well-preserved example can be seen in the Winterbourne Stoke Crossroads Barrows (see page 27).

Right: Aerial view of the two circuits of ditch at the causewayed enclosure known as Robin Hood's Ball

Facing page: A view along the Neolithic Cursus from its west end, with the Bronze-Age Cursus Barrows visible to the right

Right: A view from above of House 851, one of the Neolithic houses excavated near the eastern entrance to Durrington Walls

1 Stake holes – the traces of small upright timbers, part of wattle walls originally rendered with chalky clay

2 Floor – made of chalk, beaten flat and worn smooth by human feet

3 Hearth – each house has one

4 Slots for horizontal wooden boards, the traces of wooden beds, cupboards and other furniture ranged between the walls of the house and the chalk foor

5 Pits – containing pottery, animal bone and flints. They were dug through or outside the house and may have been part of rituals to do with the abandonment of the house

Below: This pot, found at Durrington Walls, is in the distinctive style known as Grooved Ware, often associated with Neolithic henge monuments (now in the Salisbury and South Wiltshire Museum)

DURRINGTON WALLS

Just before 2500 BC, when the great stones were being brought to Stonehenge, other henges – enclosures of chalk and timber – were being built within the surrounding landscape. The greatest of these was Durrington Walls, a massive enclosure over 470m (500yds) in diameter on the west bank of the river Avon nearly 3km (2 miles) north-east of Stonehenge. Durrington is a more traditional henge, with a huge bank lying outside an equally massive ditch, but despite its size it is difficult to see from ground level.

There are four entrances to the enclosure, the most obvious one pointing south-east down towards the river. Excavations carried out between 1966 and 1968 revealed the ditch to be over 6m (20ft) deep and 13m (43ft) wide and uncovered the remains of two circles of timber posts, the largest 23m (75ft) in diameter.

More recent excavations, from 2004 onwards, have shown that, like Stonehenge, Durrington has an avenue: a gravelled pathway, also with a solstice alignment, which runs from the southern timber circle through the south-eastern entrance and down to the river Avon. Close to this avenue – and preserved under the huge henge bank –

clusters of small rectangular Neolithic houses were discovered. These date from about 2500 BC and each was about 5m (17ft) across, with walls of wooden stakes and clay daub, and inside a rectangular floor of hard packed chalk, in the centre of which was a hearth. The space between the chalk floor and the outer wall may have been filled with wooden beds and cupboards. The rubbish that had piled up against the fences that separated the houses included huge quantities of animal bone, mostly young pig, suggesting large-scale feasting, particularly in mid-winter.

It is possible that there were hundreds of houses at Durrington in about 2500 BC, making this the largest Neolithic village in Britain and Ireland. Although probably only occupied at certain times of the year, these may be the dwellings of the people who built and used Stonehenge. Other, more special houses, surrounded by deep ditches, like smaller henges, were found inside the main henge enclosure. The evidence of both everyday life and ceremony from excavation suggests that the houses and the great timber circles were built first, and that the huge ditch and bank that encircled and in some places covered them were a later addition.

WOODHENGE

Close to Durrington Walls lies Woodhenge, a site that aerial photographs taken in 1925 revealed to be a levelled henge. The bank and internal ditch enclosed a circular area about 50m (160ft) in diameter, with a single entrance facing north-east. Within the interior lay six concentric circles of pits, varying considerably in size and shown by excavations carried out shortly after the discovery to have held upright timbers. Because of the similarity of this plan to that of Stonehenge, this site became known as Woodhenge.

Because there is only a ground plan, these timber circles are as difficult to interpret as those from Durrington Walls. The upright timbers may have stood in the open air, either plain or highly decorated. They may have been linked together by horizontal beams to create a wooden version of Stonehenge or may even have been the framework for a huge building.

Finds of decorated Grooved Ware pottery and other artefacts were discovered in specific locations within the site and suggest that the interior of the enclosure was used in an ordered way. Perhaps the most disturbing find was a grave that lay under a small flint cairn in the centre of the site. This contained the skeleton of a child aged about three, suggested by the excavator as having had its skull split open. Woodhenge, which was built in about 2300 BC, is now in the care of English Heritage and has unrestricted visitor access. There is a car park and the excavated post holes are marked by coloured concrete pillars.

CONEYBURY HENGE

Another henge lies on the summit of Coneybury Hill, 1.4km (0.8 miles) to the south-east of Stonehenge. This site, though at first thought to be a ploughed round barrow, was shown on aerial photographs of the 1970s to be a small henge, an oval enclosure with a single north-east-facing entrance. This entrance alignment is shared with Stonehenge and Woodhenge. Excavations in 1980 showed that the ditch was deep and steep-sided, and that pits containing Grooved Ware pottery lay within the interior. Coneybury was built in about 2700 BC, an early date for a henge monument. It is not visible from ground level, but the site can be viewed from a nearby path.

WEST AMESBURY HENGE

A remarkable discovery made in 2008 was that Stonehenge's Avenue ends, not at the water's edge at the river Avon, but at another small henge. Here a circular ditch with traces of an external bank, now partly washed away by the river, encloses a circle of deep pits. These have been suggested as originally containing upright stones, perhaps even some of the bluestones that were eventually set up at Stonehenge. Whatever stood in these pits was removed in about 2500 BC and only then was the ditch and bank of the henge itself built.

Below left: An artist's impression of Woodhenge as it may have appeared during its period of use
Below: Two chalk axes (symbolic rather than functional) that were discovered during excavations at Woodhenge (now in the Wiltshire Heritage Museum, Devizes)

Barrow Types

Each Bronze-Age round barrow was the tomb of an individual, accompanied to the next world with personal possessions, including ornaments of exotic materials such as jet, amber and gold

Within the Stonehenge landscape the most numerous and spectacular prehistoric monuments are undoubtedly the great groups of round barrows. These are Bronze-Age burial mounds of a wide variety of shapes and sizes, dating from the time when Stonehenge was being rebuilt in stone.

Unlike the earlier, Neolithic long barrows that contain groups of burials, each Bronze-Age round barrow was the tomb of an individual. Their remains were either buried or cremated and they were accompanied to the next world with a wide variety of personal possessions, including pottery vessels, tools of stone, bone or bronze, and ornaments of exotic materials such as jet, amber and gold.

When first built, the gleaming white chalk mounds of these barrows would have been highly visible in the landscape, especially when positioned on prominent ridges and hills. Many of the fine barrow groups that surround Stonehenge lie on National Trust open access land (see map on page 29).

1 Bowl barrows can vary in size considerably. They have a mound usually surrounded by a ditch

2 Bell barrows have a flat or slightly sloping area separating the mound and the surrounding ditch

3 Disc barrows have a small mound lying within a flat circular area surrounded by a ditch and an external bank

4 Saucer barrows have a low mound surrounded by a ditch and external bank

5 Pond barrows, an extremely rare form, have a shallow circular hollow surrounded by a low bank

THE BARROW GROUPS

The great concentration of Bronze-Age round barrows around Stonehenge attracted the attention of antiquaries and pioneering archaeologists. In the early years of the 19th century hundreds of barrows were excavated by William Cunnington, a self-taught archaeologist working under the patronage of Sir Richard Colt Hoare, a wealthy Wiltshire landowner. Their digging methods seem crude by today's standards. Experience taught them that each barrow had a central burial, so a hole was dug straight down until the burial was found. They did identify different types of barrow, and recorded in some detail what they found while digging. They also mapped the landscape – the area that Colt Hoare called the Stonehenge Environs – and gave names that are still used today to many of the barrow groups.

They published their findings promptly, illustrated with detailed engravings, and were fascinated by the objects that had been placed in the grave – the pottery vessels, the weapons and tools of bronze and the ornaments and jewellery of bone, gold, jet and amber. The human remains were of no interest and were replaced in the grave. The only barrows to escape the attentions of Colt Hoare and Cunnington were the King Barrows, on the ridge to the east of Stonehenge. These had trees growing on them at the time and the landowner was not willing to cut them down, so these are the only barrows in the immediate landscape around Stonehenge to retain their burials intact.

The Cursus Barrows

As the name of this group suggests, it lies close to the Cursus, on the crest of a low ridge that runs parallel to its southern bank. This position is quite deliberate: the mounds of the impressive bowl and bell barrows are placed so that they are most prominent and, from Stonehenge, appear silhouetted against the skyline. In 1723 the antiquary William Stukeley investigated some of the barrows in this group, finding cremated human bones and beads of amber and glass that led him to believe he had found the grave of a young woman. In 1803 the barrows were re-examined by Colt Hoare and Cunnington, who found more burials and some fine pottery vessels. The Cursus Barrows lie on National Trust open access land.

The Winterbourne Stoke Crossroads Barrows

The earliest barrow in this group is a Neolithic long barrow, the alignment of which was followed, perhaps more than a thousand years later, by a line of large bowl and bell barrows. Then, over several hundred more years, as burial fashions changed in the earlier part of the Bronze Age (between about 2000 and 1600 BC) other, more elaborate, barrow types were added. There are smaller bowl barrows, disc barrows and saucer barrows, their beautiful but shallow forms best appreciated from the air. There are even examples of rare pond barrows.

Almost all the barrows in this group were excavated in the early 19th century, the most spectacular finds being the remains of two wooden coffins, many decorated pottery vessels and spearheads and daggers of bronze. This spectacular and well-preserved barrow group has a burial history that may span as much as 2,000 years and contains every type of round barrow to be found in southern England. The Winterbourne Stoke Crossroads Barrows are partly owned by the National Trust and partly privately owned; they can be seen from a nearby path.

The New King Barrows

To the east of Stonehenge, a group of large mounds can be seen among the trees that lie on the crest of the closest ridge. These are the New King Barrows, part of a group (with the Old King Barrows to the north) that meanders along the ridge for a distance of over 1km (0.6 miles).

The New King barrow group contains some of the largest bowl and bell barrows within the Stonehenge landscape and it is the only group that was not excavated in the 19th century, because even at that time it was protected by a covering of trees. The only clues about the date and structure of the barrows have come from holes torn in the mounds when some of the trees on the ridge were toppled by storms in 1990. These suggested that some of the mounds were of an unusual construction, built largely of turf and capped with chalk from the surrounding ditch.

There is no firm evidence for when the New King Barrows were built, but their sheer size suggests that they may be of an early date for round barrows, perhaps raised between 2300 and 2000 BC. The New King Barrows are visible from a nearby path.

Left: Aerial photograph of the Winterbourne Stoke Crossroads barrow group, with the Neolithic long barrow at the top right
Far left: The Cursus Barrows seen from the air

Above: A gold breast plate (upper) and belt hook (lower) from Bush Barrow (all the finds from Bush Barrow are now in the Wiltshire Heritage Museum, Devizes)
Right: The Normanton Down barrows. Beyond the two magnificent disc barrows, and crowned with a single bush, lies Bush Barrow, where spectacular finds were made in 1808
Below: Two bronze daggers and a bronze axe with the reconstructed sceptre (centre), from Bush Barrow

The Normanton Down Barrows

The Normanton Down barrows lie along the crest of a low ridge just to the south of Stonehenge. They were described by the early 19th-century antiquary Sir Richard Colt Hoare as 'a noble group – diversified in their forms, perfect in their symmetry, and rich in their contents'.

Within the group there are some spectacularly large disc barrows, called 'Druid barrows' by Colt Hoare and his digging collaborator William Cunnington. The finds that they produced,

including beads and other personal ornaments, convinced them that they were the burial places of females. Colt Hoare's comments about 'rich' barrows were largely due to the finds made in a large mound known as Bush Barrow in 1808.

Cunnington had first investigated this mound without result on 11 July but returned in September and found 'the skeleton of a stout and tall man, lying from north to south'. He also found an amazing group of objects, including bronze daggers still with the remains of their wooden handles. These were decorated with complex patterns made up of minute gold pins. There was a bronze axe and what may have been a stone-headed sceptre with bone decorations to its handle. But the most spectacular finds were three objects – a breast plate, a smaller lozenge-shaped sheet and a belt hook – all made of pure gold. Bush Barrow is the richest single burial in the immediate vicinity of Stonehenge.

The Normanton Down Barrows are privately owned but Bush Barrow and the adjacent disc barrows can be viewed from nearby paths.

The Stonehenge World Heritage Site

Many of the monuments around Stonehenge can be visited; for a virtual tour of the World Heritage Site, look up the English Heritage Stonehenge web pages

Of the many prehistoric monuments in the Stonehenge World Heritage Site, only Woodhenge is, like Stonehenge, in the care of English Heritage. It is a free site with a dedicated car park and can be visited at any reasonable time. Many of the other prehistoric monuments in the World Heritage Site are on land owned by the National Trust. Open access on foot (not confined to public rights of way) is permitted in the area shown on the map. The National Trust is working towards increasing the proportion of its land classified as open access – visitors can obtain up-to-date details by calling **01980 664780**.

The rest of the World Heritage Site is in private ownership and access is restricted to public rights of way. Many of the paths are unsurfaced and weather conditions affect their quality. Gates, stiles and cattle grids are all present at different points. Many of the monuments have been eroded over time and are no longer visible from ground level. Interpretation panels are provided for some key features and are indicated (to the left) by a * sign.

1 Stonehenge
2 The Avenue *
3 The Cursus *
4 The Lesser Cursus
5 Durrington Walls *
6 Woodhenge *
7 Coneybury Henge *
8 West Amesbury Henge
9 The Cursus Barrows *
10 Winterbourne Stoke Crossroads Barrows *
11 New King Barrows *
12 Normanton Down Barrows *

Key

 World Heritage Site

National Trust open access land

Archaeological sites

Main roads

Minor roads

Byways, bridleways and footpaths

National Trust permissive paths

History of Stonehenge

From its earliest phase up to its abandonment 1,500 years later, Stonehenge was probably the most important temple in Britain. Since then, it has been viewed by different ages and by different people both as an enigma and as a source of inspiration. From the Middle Ages onwards, people have been trying to understand the origins of Stonehenge and answer the fundamental questions about how and why it was built. New excavations and the reanalysis of previous finds have continually changed the way the site and its landscape are interpreted and these changes will continue. So what follows is not the final answer: it is simply our current state of understanding.

READING THE HISTORY

This section outlines the history of Stonehenge from the earliest earthwork enclosure to the completed stone monument, setting each stage in its changing landscape. A description of the site from its final phase up to the present day follows, beginning on page 40.

BEFORE STONEHENGE

Stonehenge was not the first structure to be built on this part of Salisbury Plain. Excavations carried out in 1966 and 1989 in the area of the present car park revealed four large pits, all of which showed convincing evidence that they had originally held large timber posts of about 75cm (30in) in diameter. The wood that was used for the posts was identified as pine – an unusual tree to be found on chalk soils – but the date of the posts was even more unexpected. Radiocarbon dating showed that this was between 8500 and 7000 BC, in a period known as the Mesolithic, or Middle Stone Age. This was not long after the end of the last Ice Age, when Britain was still connected to mainland Europe.

As sea levels rose in the warming climate, trees grew: initially pine and hazel. Within this forest, in river valleys and on seashores, bands of hunters and gatherers lived on wild foods. It was these people who raised the posts, perhaps best interpreted as poles of the kind found on Native North American sites, commonly known as totem poles. These structures, more than 9,000 years old and built so close to Stonehenge, are unique.

There is nothing else like them in the British Isles from this ancient time.

Several thousand years later, by about 4000 BC, people had begun to tame the wildwood – the mixed forest of elm, oak and hazel that had replaced the earlier pine forests over much of mainland Britain. Using stone axes to fell trees and fires to create clearings, they opened up spaces in which they could farm. Unlike farming today, with its large fields and neat hedges, small cleared areas were carved out of the woods to grow cereals such as wheat and barley; there were also domesticated animals: cattle, pigs and sheep.

Farming, even on a small scale, brings stability and ties people to the land; it was at this time, between about 4000 and 3000 BC, that communal efforts resulted in the building of the first ceremonial monuments and burial mounds. Some upland chalk areas, like that around Stonehenge, may have had more of these sites because they remained comparatively free of woodland. The causewayed enclosure known as Robin Hood's Ball, to the north-west of Stonehenge, was built at this time, as were both Cursus monuments and probably most of the long barrows in the area.

Below: Prehistoric finds from the area around Salisbury Plain dating from the time of the first Stonehenge or just before

Facing page: One of the standing sarsen stones carved with graffiti by generations of visitors

1 Antler tools from before the time of Stonehenge, used for working leather and textiles (now in the Alexander Keiller Museum)

2 Three stone tools found in a Neolithic pottery vessel; the curved one is a flint sickle and provides rare evidence of agriculture at this time (now in the Salisbury and South Wiltshire Museum)

3 Polished flint axes from the period before Stonehenge was built

4 Early Neolithic pots with a baggy shape that may imitate the leather vessels more commonly used before this period

(Artefact groups 3 and 4 are now in the Wiltshire Heritage Museum, Devizes)

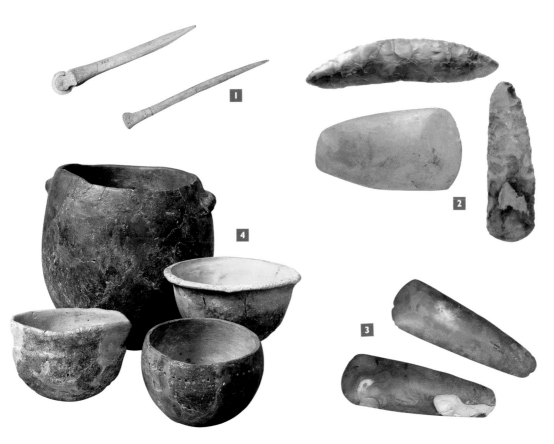

Timeline of Stonehenge

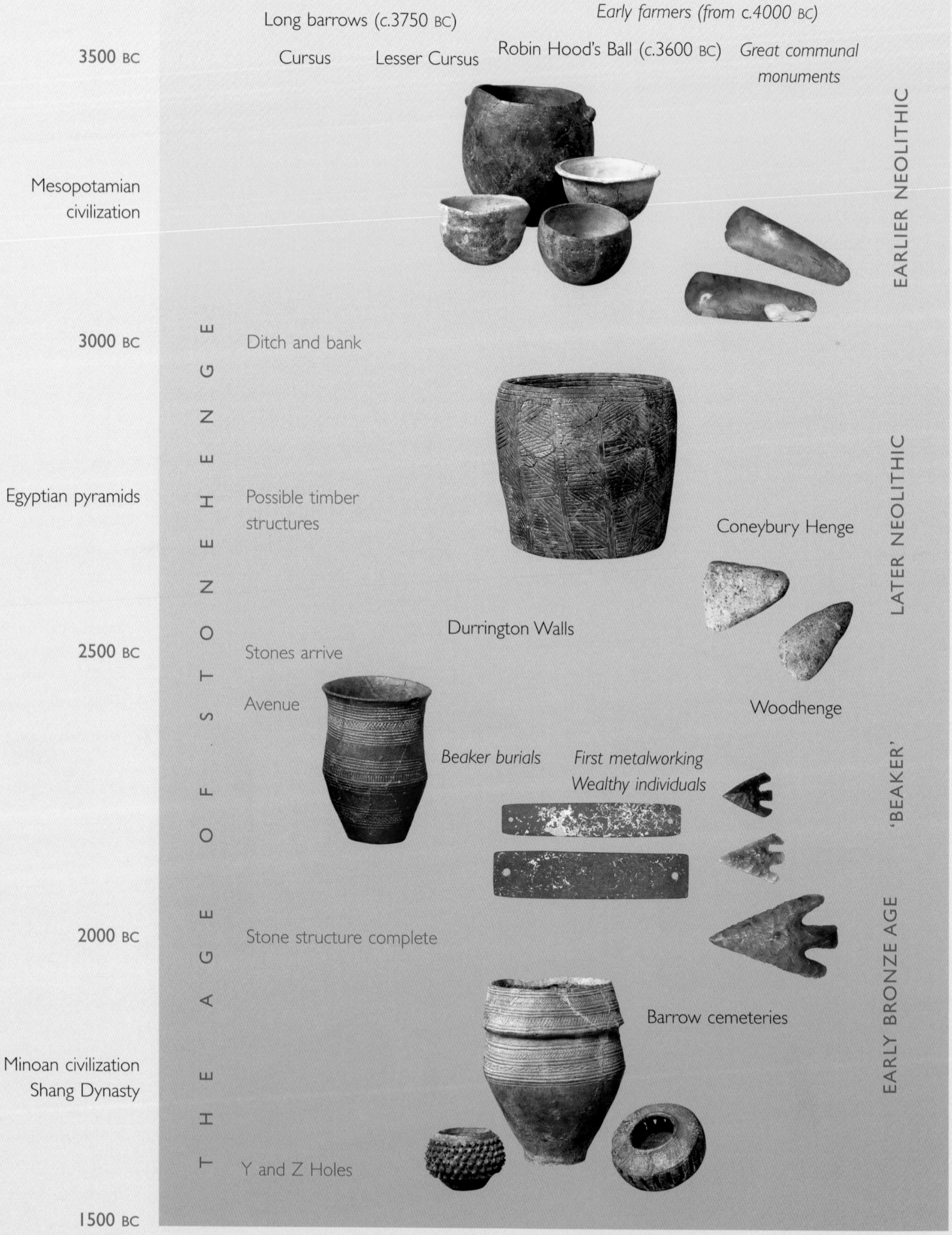

Long barrows (c.3750 BC)   Early farmers (from c.4000 BC)

3500 BC   Cursus   Lesser Cursus   Robin Hood's Ball (c.3600 BC)   Great communal
monuments

EARLIER NEOLITHIC

Mesopotamian
civilization

3000 BC   Ditch and bank

Egyptian pyramids   Possible timber
structures

Coneybury Henge

LATER NEOLITHIC

Durrington Walls

2500 BC   Stones arrive

Avenue   Woodhenge

Beaker burials   First metalworking
Wealthy individuals

'BEAKER'

2000 BC   Stone structure complete

Barrow cemeteries

Minoan civilization
Shang Dynasty

EARLY BRONZE AGE

Y and Z Holes

1500 BC

THE AGE OF STONEHENGE

THE FIRST STONEHENGE

The first Stonehenge was an enclosure, its slightly sloping central area defined by an irregularly dug ditch with an interior bank of a more regular profile. Around parts of the ditch was a small outer, or counterscarp, bank. There were two certain entrances. One faced north-east and remained in use throughout the active life of Stonehenge, while a smaller one faced south. The position of the main entrance was crucial to the function of Stonehenge, as it faced towards the midsummer sunrise in one direction, and aligned with the midwinter sunset in the other. This alignment was deliberate, and suggests that Stonehenge, from its earliest phase, was concerned with the movements of the sun.

The size of the ditch and the volume of material that it would have produced suggest that the bank could have stood as much as 2m (6.5ft) high. The irregularity of the ditch suggests that it may have merely been a quarry to provide chalk, with the bank being more important. The digging of the ditch can be radiocarbon dated, using samples from antler picks found on its floor, to between 3000 and 2920 BC. Cattle bones also found in the base of the ditch were found to be as much as 300 years older. These bones, perhaps the relics from ancient ceremonies, suggest that this had been a special place even before the enclosure was built.

The construction of the enclosure was clearly a communal effort, and it is possible that individual sections of the ditch were dug by different groups of people. Small bands of individuals, families or tribal groups, may have come from some distance to work together on this great project. It is less certain what, if anything, was taking place inside the enclosure at this time.

Recent excavations have provided the first clues as to why Stonehenge is located where it is. The Avenue may originally have been marked by parallel natural gullies created at the end of the last Ice Age, which were visible in the landscape and coincidentally aligned on the winter and summer solstices. There is also the possibility that the Heel Stone is a rare local sarsen, discovered very close to where it now stands. A combination of these two striking natural phenomena may well have provided the impetus for the work that followed.

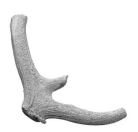

Above: One of the antler picks used in the digging of the Stonehenge ditch in about 3000 BC (now in the Salisbury and South Wiltshire Museum)
Below: The first Stonehenge, a simple earthwork enclosure – the result of great communal effort – being constructed

Midsummer sunrise

Midwinter sunset

THE TIMBER PHASE

The earthwork enclosure probably did not stay empty for long. Twentieth-century excavations at Stonehenge have all revealed holes dug into the chalk that once held upright wooden posts of varying size. Few are dated and, although in the illustration above they are shown together as part of a timber phase, pre-dating the arrival of the stones, it is possible that some may date to later stages of Stonehenge's development.

Around the inner edge of the bank were 56 regularly spaced pits, the Aubrey Holes, which can be shown to date to this early phase. These may have held wooden posts or, as suggested by some early excavators and again after the re-excavation of one of them in 2008, small upright stones.

In the main entrance to the enclosure and immediately outside this entrance were regular rows of smaller posts and from the second, southern entrance parallel rows of close-set posts, perhaps part of a fenced entrance passage, wound their way towards the centre of the enclosure. This is the area where it could reasonably be expected that the most important wooden structures would have stood. Unfortunately this is where, in later years, the raising of the stones obliterated the subtle traces of holes for wooden posts. What remain are hints of what may have been either a circular structure or a number of rectangular structures.

What is more definite is that, at some time during this phase, Stonehenge became a place of burial. Many deposits of cremated human bone have been found during excavations, almost all round the outside of the enclosure. They were found in the partly-filled ditch, cut into and just inside the bank, and in the upper levels of the Aubrey Holes which, by this time, appear to have had their uprights removed.

The majority of the cremations were found in the 1920s by Colonel William Hawley. In 1935, his assistant Robert Newall, without any means of understanding their significance, reburied them in a previously excavated Aubrey Hole. As some of these burial deposits included ash and charcoal from funeral pyres, it is likely that the actual cremations took place quite close by. Few objects accompany the cremated bones, but a number of long pins of antler or animal bone show evidence of having been burnt, presumably along with the body. There is also a highly polished stone mace-head, clearly a much-prized possession.

Midsummer sunrise

Midwinter sunset

THE EARLY STONE PHASE

The next stage in the development of Stonehenge saw its transformation, some time just before 2500 BC, from a simple enclosure to something quite different. Stones arrived: sarsens from the Marlborough Downs, and a much greater number of bluestones from the Preseli Hills in Wales.

Four small sarsens, now known as the Station Stones, were set upright just inside the inner edge of the bank. Immediately outside the enclosure entrance were two larger sarsens, the surviving example now known as the Heel Stone.

The bluestones were first set up in a peculiar arrangement that is only known from excavation. Two concentric arcs of stone holes, known as the Q and R Holes, were found on the northern and eastern sides of the central area of the site. The base of each hole showed the impression of a large stone, in which minute chips of bluestone were embedded. This setting is difficult to interpret. The arcs of stone holes may have been part of a circular structure, but few traces of it have been found on what would have been its southern and western sides. It does, however, reflect the axis of the enclosure: multiple stone holes on its north-eastern side pointing in this

highly significant direction. The precise date of this stone setting is unknown, although it must have been built at an early stage as both Q and R Holes are cut through by holes dug to take stones of the later bluestone circle.

Although the bluestones all come from the Preseli Hills, they include many different types of rock. Some are attractive blue-greens or blue-greys, sometimes flecked or spotted with white, others are soft and dull-looking. So why was this miscellaneous collection of stones brought from Wales to Salisbury Plain?

Perhaps what arrived were the components of a complete stone circle that had stood in Wales. Here each stone, attractive or not, would have been special. In this and in all their subsequent rearrangements, the bluestones appear to have stood as single upright pillars. But evidence of worn mortise and tenon joints on some of them suggest that they may have stood as parts of miniature bluestone trilithons.

No trace of this arrangement of bluestones can be seen today. The stones were removed and their holes packed with chalk. But what accompanied them did survive – the massive sarsen circle and the trilithons.

Top: The construction of the double bluestone circle at Stonehenge, envisaged here as constructed before the larger sarsens arrived, some time just before 2500 BC
***Above:** A fine battle-axe made from Preseli bluestone, from a barrow south of Stonehenge (now in the Salisbury and South Wiltshire Museum)*

Above: Three finely worked flint arrowheads, part of the equipment introduced alongside Beaker pots and the first metals (now in the Salisbury and South Wiltshire Museum)

Below: Stonehenge in about 2300 BC, showing the final form of the sarsen circle and trilithons – a massive feat of engineering

THE LATE STONE PHASE

Some time later, minor changes took place around the outer parts of the monument. A circular ditch was dug around the Heel Stone and its companion stone was removed. Three stones were raised in a line across the entrance causeway, the Slaughter Stone, now fallen, being the sole survivor. Two of the Station Stones were also surrounded by low, ditched mounds, known as the North and South Barrows.

What spectacularly changed Stonehenge, however, was the arrival, shaping and raising of the 75 sarsens that go to form the outer circle and the horseshoe of massive trilithons. This seems to have happened in about 2500 BC, but over what length of time this major construction took place is unknown. There is also a lack of archaeological evidence to show in which order the two main structures were built. Logic suggests that the horseshoe of trilithons was built first, or at least before the outer circle was finished – whether it ever was completed is uncertain. Much of it is now missing and there is one upright on its southern side that would never have reached the required height to support a lintel. Perhaps the

supply of suitable stones simply ran out before the structure was completed. Finished or not, in its original form the outer circle must have been an extremely elegant structure. The gently curved lintels were beautifully shaped and jointed and the upper surface of the stone ring that they formed was almost exactly level, even though Stonehenge is built on a slope.

Equally elegant and even more massive were the five sarsen trilithons, graduated in size from the shortest that lay at the open end of the horseshoe to the tallest, the Great Trilithon, that stood facing the enclosure entrance. This horseshoe re-emphasized the alignment of the whole temple, originally established by the position of the entrance into the earthwork enclosure. It is possible that the bluestones still stood in their Q and R Hole settings or indeed that they were raised at the same time as these great sarsen structures.

The completion of the sarsen circle and trilithon horseshoe marked the end of a massive undertaking for the builders of Stonehenge. Their engineering on a monumental scale had created the most iconic prehistoric structure in the world.

Midsummer sunrise

Midwinter sunset

THE FINAL PHASE

Further changes took place between 2300 and 2000 BC when once again the stones that lay in and close to the enclosure's entrance were repositioned. It is at this time, if not earlier, as suggested by recent archaeological evidence, that the line of the entrance was extended down the sloping hillside by the twin ditches and banks of the Avenue.

This is also when the bluestones, those that had stood in the double bluestone circle (the Q and R Hole setting), with the possible addition of stones from elsewhere, were rearranged. As many as 60 of them were set up in a circle just inside and concentric with the outer sarsen circle. Inside the horseshoe of sarsen trilithons more bluestones, the tallest and most elegantly shaped pillars, were set up, initially to form an oval. At a later date, perhaps even as late as Roman times, stones were removed from the north-eastern end of the oval, leaving the inner bluestone horseshoe of today.

The creation of these new bluestone settings also involved the placing of the Altar Stone at the closed end of the bluestone horseshoe, in the shadow of the Great Trilithon. This finely worked slab of greenish sandstone from south Wales is the largest of the non-sarsen stones. It may have stood as a wide pillar at the focal point of the central stone settings, or may have lain flat, as a real altar. With the exception of the Y and Z Holes, dug just outside the sarsen circle perhaps as late as 1600 BC, this was the end of construction at Stonehenge.

Much of this effort, over more than 1,000 years, was to create a temple to the sun. Built into the structure of Stonehenge from the very beginning was one fundamental alignment. The line that runs out from the open end of the stone horseshoes, through the entrance and down the first part of the Avenue, marks the position of the rising sun at midsummer and, perhaps more importantly, of the setting sun at midwinter.

What rituals may have been carried out at these times can only be guessed at, but it is likely that only the most important people would have been allowed within the stones themselves. Here, partly hidden from those who had travelled to be part of the great occasion, they would have carried out ceremonies to ensure that the seasons changed.

Above: Bronze daggers of the Early Bronze Age, when Stonehenge was in its final phase (now in the Wiltshire Heritage Museum, Devizes)
Below: A Winter Solstice gathering during the final phase of Stonehenge in about 2000 BC

Midsummer sunrise

Midwinter sunset

PEOPLE OF STONEHENGE

The 1,000 years before construction started at Stonehenge had seen great changes in peoples' lives, as farming gradually replaced a life of hunting and gathering wild foods on these rolling chalk uplands. This change meant settling down and investing in land, with the consequent ideas of ownership and territory. This was the time, in the earlier part of the Neolithic era (or New Stone Age), when tools were made of wood, stone or bone and when simple pottery vessels were made and used. It was also when long barrows and causewayed enclosures were built, communal monuments whose existence suggest an organized society, the presence of leadership, and the ability to communicate with large and possibly far-flung communities. The increasing emphasis on farming would also have ensured regular food supplies, freeing up part of the labour force for these essentially non-productive activities.

Stonehenge was built and presumably used over a period of at least 1,400 years, a huge length of time that saw considerable changes in the way prehistoric people lived their lives. The simple earthwork enclosure was started towards the end of the Neolithic era but we know little of the people who built it. We know more of the everyday lives of those who raised the stones nearly 500 years later, as their small, neatly built houses have been found at Durrington Walls. From these it is possible to learn more about their diet, and perhaps the organization of their society.

There are, however, three remarkable human burials, discovered at Stonehenge itself and nearby, which provide a fascinating insight into the great changes that were taking place at the time the stones were being raised.

In 1976 an excavation in the ditch at Stonehenge revealed a human skeleton, buried with several finely worked flint arrowheads, some with their tips broken off, and a wrist protector made of stone, likely to have been used by an archer. The arrowheads were of Early Bronze-Age style and the man, who died in about 2300 BC, soon became known as the Stonehenge Archer.

Examination of the bones showed that he was a local, aged about 30 and that he had met a violent death. The missing tips of the flint arrowheads were found embedded in his bones, so the arrows were not his possessions but the cause of his death. But even though he died violently, perhaps as a sacrifice, he was given a

Right: Two copper knives from the Amesbury Archer burial, some of the earliest metal artefacts found in Britain
Far right: *Fine flint arrowheads buried with the Amesbury Archer*

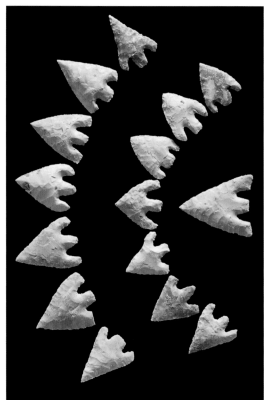

careful burial in a place that was by that time perhaps the most sacred place in the British Isles.

The discovery in May 2002 of another burial in Amesbury, about 5km (3 miles) from Stonehenge, provides a stark contrast to the one from Stonehenge. The Amesbury Archer, discovered during excavations on a building site, had the richest grave ever discovered from the time of Stonehenge. The man, aged between 35 and 45 years old, had been buried in about 2400 BC with an astonishing collection of artefacts. This was the time when the first metals, copper and gold, were being introduced from continental Europe, alongside a distinctive type of decorated pottery vessel known as Beaker ware. In his grave this man had three copper knives and no fewer than five Beaker pots, two stone wrist protectors, 16 finely worked flint arrowheads and a pair of gold hair ornaments, the earliest gold to be found in Britain. He also had what appears to be a small stone anvil. Bone analysis showed that this man was not local, but was born somewhere in the Alps, most probably in what is now Switzerland. So he may have been one of the first to introduce metalworking to Britain, a skill that would have earned him enormous prestige and wealth.

In May 2003 another extraordinary grave was discovered at Boscombe, about 6km (4 miles) from Stonehenge. Dating from about 2300 BC, it contained at least eight Beaker pots, the most ever found in a single grave. But it also contained many skeletons: three adult males, a teenage male and three children aged between two and seven years.

Their skulls suggest that they were all related and, strangely, some of the bones appeared worn, as if they had been buried previously in another place. Both pots and radiocarbon dates showed that this was a Beaker period grave, dating to the time of the first use of metal, but the method of burial was from much earlier: from the Stone Age. These men, dubbed the Boscombe Bowmen, were also from outside the local area. Analysis of isotopes in their teeth showed that they had most probably spent the first few years of their lives in Wales, the source of the Stonehenge bluestones.

These three burials from the Beaker period show the way that archaeological science can help us to understand the wider cultural influences at work in the building of Stonehenge, a truly international monument.

Above: Two stone wrist guards buried with the Amesbury Archer
Below right: Pots of the distinctive Beaker style, early examples of which date from the period when the first metals were used in Britain, in about 2300 BC
Below left: The Amesbury Archer burial, photographed during overnight excavations

AFTER STONEHENGE

Although Stonehenge was effectively completed by 1600 BC, we have no evidence to show how long after this it continued in use. But even if Stonehenge remained the same, the surrounding landscape continued to change. More and more elaborate round barrows were built, continuing the emphasis on burial, but towards the end of the Bronze Age (about 1000 BC) there is increasing evidence of everyday life.

Boundary ditches divided up the landscape and small, regular arable fields spread across land that had formerly been used mainly as pasture. The banks of the Cursus (see page 22), now more than 2,000 years old, were used as field boundaries by Bronze-Age farmers who ploughed its interior. These farmers lived in the small settlements that appeared scattered across the landscape, each a cluster of circular houses of wood and thatch, set within their fields.

Before the Roman conquest of AD 43, Stonehenge had ceased to be a living temple but it appears to have had a new lease of life under the Roman invaders. Many finds of Roman date (coins, brooches and pottery) indicate more than just casual visiting and recent excavations have shown that bluestones were being removed, or even reset, at this time. Stonehenge may have become a Roman shrine.

In about AD 645, a man was buried at Stonehenge. He had been decapitated and may have been executed as a criminal. Sometime after this the name of Stonehenge emerged, formed from the words 'stone' and 'henge', the latter meaning 'hanging' and possibly referring to the resemblance of the stones to a gallows.

From medieval times onwards much energy was expended in trying to guess the date, the builders and the purpose of Stonehenge. The first written description, dating from about 1130, appeared in Henry of Huntingdon's *History of the English People*, where he described 'Stanenges, where stones of wonderful size have been erected after the manner of doorways ... no one can conceive how such great stones have been so raised aloft, or why they were built there'.

In 1136 Geoffrey of Monmouth explained in his *History of the Kings of Britain* that Stonehenge was a memorial to a great battle between Saxons and Britons. He suggested that the stones came from an Irish stone circle called the Giants' Round, and had been transported to Salisbury Plain by the wizard Merlin. This idea proved popular and was widely accepted until as late as the 16th century.

Above: A manuscript illumination showing Merlin building Stonehenge, from a mid-14th-century adaptation of Geoffrey of Monmouth
Right: Stonehenge drawn by Lucas de Heere, a Dutch traveller, in 1574

Facing page: Stonehenge inspired generations of artists including J M W Turner (1775–1851), who produced this painting (detail)

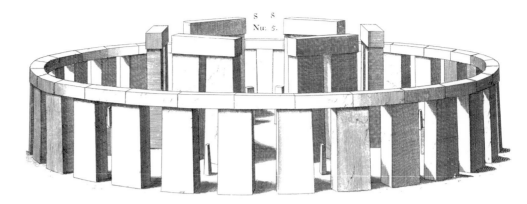

ANTIQUARIES AND ROMANTICS

Due to a renewed interest in the ancient past during the 17th century, new ways of trying to understand Stonehenge were employed. In 1629 the Duke of Buckingham had a hole dug in the centre of the monument, but was disappointed as it produced nothing more than 'stagges hornes and bulls hornes and charcoales'. While an archaeologist today would be more than satisfied with such a collection of samples for radiocarbon dating, he did not consider them of any great interest.

King James I decided that Stonehenge should be studied in detail and engaged the architect Inigo Jones (1573–1652) to carry out the work. Jones concluded that Stonehenge could not have been built by the native Britons, as they were, 'a savage and barbarous people … destitute of the knowledge … to erect stately structures or such remarkable works as Stoneheng'. Onto the plan of Stonehenge, Jones superimposed an elaborate geometrical design consisting of four equilateral triangles within a circle. He needed a degree of imagination to do this: an extra trilithon had to be added to create the required perfect symmetry,

but to Jones it was sufficient proof that Stonehenge must have been built by the Romans.

The Danes and Phoenicians soon appeared alongside the Saxons and Romans as potential builders of Stonehenge, although there were some who began to suggest that the ancient Britons were responsible. Among these was John Aubrey (1626–97), a Wiltshire-born antiquary.

He realized that it was a fruitless exercise searching for the builders of Stonehenge in written historical records because such sites were 'so exceeding old that no Bookes doe reach them'. Aubrey produced his first plan of Stonehenge in 1666. It was one of the first accurate drawings of the site ever made and on it he noted a series of 'cavities in the ground' close to the inner edge of the bank. Over 250 years later excavation proved that these depressions marked the position of large pits that were named Aubrey Holes after the man who had noticed them first. Many of Aubrey's ideas are fanciful but he did conclude correctly that Stonehenge was a temple built by the ancient Britons, even though he wrongly assumed that the priests attending the temple were Druids.

Top: Portrait of John Aubrey (1626–97), a Wiltshire-born antiquary who produced the first plan of Stonehenge (engraving by Van den Gucht)
Above: *William Stukeley, who first noticed the Avenue and the Cursus, after a painting by Sir Godfrey Kneller, 1721*
Above right and right: *Stonehenge by Inigo Jones, drawn as he imagined its original geometric design (above), and in its rugged reality (right)*

John Aubrey's ideas were taken up in the early 18th century by William Stukeley, a Lincolnshire-born doctor and pioneering field archaeologist. He had the great advantage of seeing the downland that surrounded Stonehenge before much of it was ploughed up, and was the first to notice not only the Avenue leading up to Stonehenge, but also the Cursus, a long Neolithic earthwork just to the north of Stonehenge (see page 22). Stukeley also coined the term trilithon (from the Greek for three stones), to describe the arrangement of two uprights capped by a horizontal lintel. Unfortunately, however, Stukeley too became obsessed with the idea of Stonehenge being a Druid temple, and this coloured many of his later observations.

On 3 January 1797 an entire trilithon collapsed. This was the first recorded fall of stones at Stonehenge. Amongst those who visited at this time was William Cunnington (1758–1810) who went on to investigate many of the barrows that surround Stonehenge, together with his fellow archaeologist, Sir Richard Colt Hoare (1758–1838). But although the two men applied increasingly scientific methods to their investigations, Stonehenge remained a mystery. Colt Hoare, in his *Ancient History of Wiltshire*, described it in the following words: 'How Grand! How wonderful! How incomprehensible!'

It may have been incomprehensible to Colt Hoare, but to many artists of the 18th and 19th centuries Stonehenge was an inspiration. Its rugged stones were the epitome of the picturesque ruin: wild, romantic and often placed not in its rather plain downland setting but in wild and imaginary Druid-inhabited landscapes.

In 1883 Stonehenge was formally recognized as a monument of national importance, protected by the newly introduced Ancient Monuments Act. In practical terms, however, nothing changed: Stonehenge remained neglected and crumbling and on 31 December 1900, the last day of the 19th century, another stone fell.

Right: Lifting a twisted lintel off the outer circle at the beginning of Colonel Hawley's excavation campaign in 1919

Below: William Gowland's careful excavation at the base of the tallest sarsen in 1901. His workmen are sieving the soil to recover the smallest finds

MODERN INVESTIGATIONS

The fall of the stone at Stonehenge changed attitudes towards the monument, marking its move not only into the 20th century, but from ruin to national treasure. The year 1901 saw both protest at Stonehenge, as the site was fenced off for the first time, and the first restoration work.

The sole surviving upright of the Great Trilithon, which had been leaning at a precarious angle, was straightened and firmly bedded in concrete. The engineering work was accompanied by an excavation, carried out to a high standard by Professor William Gowland. He published his results very promptly, concluding that the stone had first been raised at the very end of the Stone Age or beginning of the Bronze Age, a very accurate interpretation of the evidence.

In 1915 Stonehenge was put up for auction and sold for £6,600 to Cecil Chubb, a local man, who shortly afterwards presented it to the nation. By 1919 the condition of Stonehenge was once again causing concern and more restoration was planned, this time on a grander scale.

An experienced archaeologist, Colonel William Hawley, was brought in to work alongside the engineers, but he had an additional task: to excavate the whole of Stonehenge. He dug there from 1919, starting on the sarsen circle where several leaning stones were winched to an upright position before being set in concrete. He dug for the next six years, often working alone, and

excavated many of the Aubrey Holes, about half of the ditch and a considerable part of the eastern side of the interior of the enclosure. But, although the restoration had made Stonehenge safe once more, the excavations, the results of which were never properly analysed or published, had been far from satisfactory.

In 1950 archaeologists returned to Stonehenge. Professors Richard Atkinson and Stuart Piggott and the Wiltshire archaeologist J F S Stone took up the

challenge of preparing Hawley's findings for publication, but also felt that some additional excavation was needed. They began by excavating two more Aubrey Holes, one of which provided a sample of charcoal for the first radiocarbon date for Stonehenge. The date, sometime between 2123 and 1575 BC, was rather imprecise, but it marked a real breakthrough. For the first time, Stonehenge had been dated scientifically.

Annual excavations continued until 1958, when another major engineering project began: to raise the entire trilithon that had fallen in 1797. This involved freeing the great fallen stones from the earth and moving them to storage before archaeological excavations could be carried out. Atkinson and his colleagues were able to investigate the shape of the original holes dug to receive the stones, providing important clues about how the stones had originally been raised. Finally the replaced uprights were set in concrete and the lintel was replaced. The trilithon stood again and the ruins of Stonehenge were now far easier to understand. Excavations carried on until 1964, but once again no reports were written and it was not until 1995 that the results of all the 20th-century excavations were finally published.

In 2008 two separate excavations were carried out at Stonehenge itself, small by the standards of previous investigations, but both highly significant. In May Professors Tim Darvill and Geoff Wainwright excavated a small trench on the line of the original bluestone setting, hoping to obtain firm dating evidence. Instead they discovered evidence for the deliberate destruction of and removal of bluestones during the Roman period, the first clues that Stonehenge was actively used at this time. In August Professor Mike Parker-Pearson re-excavated the cremated human remains first discovered by Colonel Hawley but reburied in 1935. These are still being studied but appear to show that the majority of the burials were of adult men and their eventual radiocarbon dating will show for how long Stonehenge was used as a place of burial.

As the understanding of Stonehenge changed during the 20th century, so too did its appearance and the way it was managed. Although first fenced off in 1901, members of the public could wander among the stones for many years after this. In 1963 the interior was gravelled in order to reduce

erosion but by 1978 the numbers of visitors had risen so high that it was decided to restrict access to the stones. The centre was grassed over and the line of an old track through the earthwork enclosure was surfaced, to allow visitors a good view of the stones.

In 1986 Stonehenge was inscribed, along with Avebury, on the prestigious World Heritage list, in recognition of the outstanding prehistoric remains at both sites and in their surrounding landscapes.

Above: Professor Richard Atkinson and his team excavating the bluestone circle in 1954
Left: Professors Tim Darvill and Geoff Wainwright excavating in 2008; their dig yielded the unexpected evidence that Stonehenge had been used during the Roman period

Local Perspectives

Isaac Crook, my grandfather, was the underbidder to Stonehenge in the big sale of 1915: he bid £6,500 and it was sold for £6,600 to a chap by the name of Cecil Chubb

Richard Crook, a local farmer, recalls his family's part in the sale of Stonehenge, shortly before Cecil Chubb donated the site to the nation:

'Isaac Crook, my grandfather, moved here from down the road in 1908. Isaac farmed Normanton Farm – that's why my father's called Norman. Isaac kept his pigs and horses behind Stonehenge in the Royal Flying Corps hangars – it still miffs me that they flattened seven tumuli to build them.

'In 1915, there was a big sale. Isaac was the underbidder to Stonehenge. He bid £6,500 – and it was sold for £6,600 to a chap by the name of Cecil Chubb.

'By the Sixties, I'd left school and was running riot. One year, the news reported two incidents at Stonehenge: a custodian's cap had been nicked, and one strand of barbed wire was broken – well, I broke that, getting over the fence!

'A gang of us had been to a dance until the small hours and afterwards we went to watch the sun rise at Stonehenge. I then started work at seven. I can remember that 21 June was a hot day that year because the staff stuck my head in a water trough when I went to sleep driving a tractor.

'The best place to see the sun set on Stonehenge is from a neighbouring farm. The farmer's related to me because his son married my daughter. And my other daughter married another farmer round the stones.

'We got the job tied up pretty well. We couldn't buy it, so we married it!'

Above: Richard Crook photographed on his first birthday with his father Norman (right) and his grandfather Isaac (left)
Right: A procession of Druids in the 1950s

Facing page: This elaborate crop circle appeared in a field near Stonehenge at about the time of the Summer Solstice in 1996

STONEHENGE FOR ALL

It has been said that every age has the Stonehenge that it deserves and it is true that over the past centuries Stonehenge has been viewed by successive generations in a wide variety of ways. After the scientific advances of the 19th century, when it was realized that Stonehenge was in fact a product of native Britons, without any exotic influence, the 20th century saw a resurgence of alternative ideas. For the first time humans could look beyond their own world and so it is hardly surprising that extraterrestrial influences were seen in Stonehenge – suggestions reinforced by the appearance of mysterious crop circles in nearby fields.

In terms of function, Stonehenge has long been regarded as a temple – the prehistoric equivalent of a great cathedral – but it has also been interpreted as a symbol of commemoration for historic battles and an observatory for recording the movements of sun, moon and stars. In an age in which the computer symbolized the height of achievement it was, again, hardly surprising that Stonehenge was interpreted as an ancient computer: the pattern of its standing stones endowed with hidden meaning and mathematical significance. In recent years, Stonehenge, which had for a time been a focus of conflict centred on the summer solstice, has become a focus for celebration. To many, in an age where there is resurgence in earth religions and new paganism, Stonehenge is once again a living temple, a place where the ancient seasonal festivals and ancestors can be commemorated. So alongside the modern Druids, who have had now over a century of association with Stonehenge, people of all nations and all beliefs come to celebrate.

THE FUTURE

Today Stonehenge suffers from its surroundings. It sits on a triangle of land, bordered on two sides by busy roads that cut it off from its surrounding landscape. The facilities for visitors are basic and cramped and there is at present no space available for exhibits to explain the site, its remarkable landscape, or the many fascinating finds that have been made in the area. But plans are well underway to change this, and in the future a visit to Stonehenge will be a very different experience. English Heritage and the National Trust are working with the Highways Agency and other partners on ambitious plans to improve the Stonehenge World Heritage Site.

Unfortunately plans to place the A303 road in a bored tunnel were rejected on the grounds of cost but plans to close the A344 road, which currently runs by the stones and separates them from the Avenue are currently underway. There are also plans to grass over the current car park and to build a new visitor centre 2.5km (1.5 miles) to the east. This will provide parking, a shop, a café, educational facilities and exhibitions on Stonehenge and its landscape. A land train will transport visitors to within walking distance of the stones. This new and ambitious project will fulfil the vision for the future of the site outlined in the Stonehenge World Heritage Site Management Plan: to restore the landscape setting and the tranquillity of Stonehenge, to improve visitor access to the surrounding monuments and to protect the archaeological landscape of which Stonehenge is such an important part. This is the future that Stonehenge deserves.

So what is Stonehenge in the 21st century? It is certainly an icon, its unique stone settings instantly recognizable as symbols of solidity and ancient achievement. It is a major tourist attraction with nearly one million visitors a year, and also a site of huge archaeological and scientific importance. Centuries of study, excavation and analysis have shown when Stonehenge was built and provided clues to the identity of the builders. Experiments have offered suggestions about how the stones might have been moved, shaped and raised. As the understanding of people's lives at the time of Stonehenge increases, it also helps to explain why such huge effort was expended by our prehistoric ancestors.

But there is much that we still do not know and it is here, in Stonehenge's mystery, that part of its appeal lies. This great temple, the most magnificent prehistoric structure in the whole of Britain and Ireland, will always keep some of its secrets.

Top and above: Aerial view of the Stonehenge site today (top), above a computer-generated view showing its appearance after proposed changes
Right: *Stonehenge today*